VERY SIMPLE
GERMAN

ILLUSTRATED BY
IRENE SANDERSON

VERY SIMPLE
GERMAN

By
Waltraud Coles

Simple Books Ltd
Sandgate, Folkestone, Kent, England

VERY SIMPLE GERMAN

Simple Books Ltd
Knoll House, 35 The Crescent, Sandgate, Folkestone,
Kent, England CT20 3EE

First published 1992
© Simple Books Ltd

ISBN 1-873411-15-4

British Library Cataloguing in Publication Data

**A CIP catalogue record for this book
is available from the British Library**

Distributed in the USA & Canada by:
THE TALMAN COMPANY INC.
150 Fifth Avenue
New York, NY 10011

PF
3121
.C65
1992

Photoset in Souvenir Light 11 on 12pt
by Visual Typesetting, Harrow, Middlesex
Printed in England by BPCC Wheatons Ltd., Exeter

Contents

ACKNOWLEDGEMENTS

I am grateful to the students who tested the material, and to my colleagues, in particular to Uwe Koreik and Peter Macardle for their helpful comments.

Introduction

German is the most frequently spoken language in Europe after Russian. Some 95 million Europeans speak it as their mother tongue. As well as in Germany itself German is spoken in Austria, in a large part of Switzerland, Liechtenstein and in some parts of Luxembourg. There are also German-speaking minorities in Belgium, France, Denmark, Northern Italy and in several Eastern European countries.

As well as different regional accents there are many regional German dialects. These dialects have their own distinctive pronunciation, vocabulary and grammar. Different words for one and the same thing may be used in different areas. For example, the word for 'Saturday' is *Sonnabend* in the north of Germany, in the south it is *Samstag*. In the north and west the word for 'spring' is *Frühjahr*, in the south and east it is *Frühling*.

In most parts of Germany people will greet you with *Guten Tag*. In the south-east of the country and in Austria, however, *Grüß Gott* is the standard greeting and in Switzerland people say *Grüezi*.

'High German', i.e. the standard form of German as given here, is understood by all German speakers.

1

Peculiarities of the German Language

eine Wohnung

G erman has four letters more than the English alphabet:

ä, ö, ü, ß

The two dots above the vowels a, o and u are called an *UMLAUT*. Umlauts completely change the sound of the vowel and a vowel with an umlaut has to be treated as a separate letter.

Kuchen = cake
Küchen = kitchens

The letter **ß** equals **ss**

Straße = *STRASSE* [street]

A ll German NOUNS are spelt with an initial
CAPITAL letter.

*Markus und Helga wohnen in einer **Großstadt**.
Sie haben eine **Wohnung** mit zwei
Schlafzimmern, **Küche**, **Wohnzimmer**, **Bad** und
einen kleinen **Garten**.*

Markus and Helga live in a large city. They have a flat
with two bedrooms, kitchen, living-room, bathroom and
a small garden.

E ach German NOUN belongs to one of three
groups:

MASCULINE				
der / ein	*Garten*			garden
FEMININE				
die / eine	*Küche*	**the / a**	kitchen
NEUTER				
das / ein	*Wohnzimmer*		living-room

The form of the word itself does not signal to
which group a particular noun belongs.

I n German there is a greater variety of word
order possible than in English. The sentence
'I shall travel to Berlin next year in the summer',
can thus be translated into German:

Ich	*fahre*	*nächstes Jahr im Sommer nach Berlin.*
Nächstes Jahr	*fahre*	*ich im Sommer nach Berlin.*
Im Sommer	*fahre*	*ich nächstes Jahr nach Berlin.*
Nach Berlin	*fahre*	*ich nächstes Jahr im Sommer.*

N ote that the VERB is the only word which
does not change its place. Everything else
rotates round it.

This means that an element other than the
subject can appear in first position:

Den Mann   *beißt*   **der** Hund.

the man   bites   the dog.

But, of course, it is *not* man bites dog but the other way round! The different forms for 'the' (here: *den* and *der*) indicate which is the subject and which is the object.

Adjectives preceding nouns also have different forms:
Den alten Mann beißt der alte Hund. [alt=old]

Despite the great variety possible there are strict rules regarding word order.

In a statement (i.e. not a question) the VERB is always in position II (see above).

	II VERB	

In questions **with a 'question word'** the VERB is also in position II.

I QUESTION WORD	II VERB	

e.g.:   *Wo wohnen Sie?*
       (Literally: Where live you? → Where do you live?)
       Was kostet das?
       (Literally: What costs this? → How much does this cost?)

In questions **without a 'question word'** the VERB takes up position I.

I VERB	

e.g.: *Wohnen Sie in Berlin?*
(Literally: Live you in Berlin? → Do you live in Berlin?)
Sprechen Sie Englisch?
(Literally: Speak you English? → Do you speak English?)

If the verb consists of more than one element part of it goes to the very end of the sentence.

	II		END POSITION
Der Zug	*fährt*	*jetzt*	*ein.*
Der Zug	*fährt*	*jetzt*	*ab.*
Der Zug	*fährt*	*jetzt*	*nicht.*
Der Zug	*ist*	*jetzt*	*abgefahren.*

fährt...ein	= arrives
fährt...ab	= leaves
fährt...nicht	= runs not → does not run
ist...abgefahren	= has left

Thus the above sentences read:
The train arrives/is arriving now.
The train leaves/is leaving now.
The train does not run now.
The train has now left.

fährt...ein, fährt...ab are so-called separable verbs. In dictionaries they are given in their infinitive, i.e. basic, form: *einfahren, abfahren.*

Note that the attention span has to stretch until the very end of the sentence (when the voice comes down) since the very last word might completely change the meaning of the message.

	II		END POSITION
Ich	*verstehe*	*die Lautspre-cherdurchsage im Bahnhof*	**nicht.**

Literally: I understand the loudspeaker announcement in the station *not*. → I do *not* understand.....

There are two words used for NEGATION.
nicht = not

*Ich kenne diese Stadt **nicht**.*
I know this city **not**. = I do <u>not</u> know this city.
*Ich wohne **nicht** in Berlin.*
I live <u>not</u> in Berlin. = I do <u>not</u> live in Berlin.
Here **nicht** precedes the word it negates.

kein [+ENDING]
Ich trinke **kein**en *Whisky.*
Ich trinke **kein**e *Limonade.*
Ich trinke **kein** *Bier.*
I drink <u>no</u> = I do <u>not</u> drink whisky/lemonade/beer.

The word for 'no' is **nein**.

Compound words are characteristic of German. Two or more words are simply joined up into one.

Öffnungszeiten

Öffnung / s / zeiten
↓ ↓
opening   times → hours of business

Geldwechselautomat

Geld / wechsel / automat
↓ ↓ ↓
money   change   machine → change
machine

The last component of a compound word gives the basic general meaning of the whole word. The word/s preceding it qualify the basic meaning and give further information.

Flughafenrestaurantmanager

Flughafen / restaurant / manager

↓
manager. What sort
of manager?
↓
restaurant → restaurant manager.
↓

What sort of restaurant?

airport → airport restaurant → airport restaurant manager.

There are two forms of address in German:
The familiar form **du** used for family members, close friends and children,

the polite form **Sie** used for everybody else.

Here the polite form only is given.

Whilst in English only he/she/it has its own distinctive verb ending(s) German has distinctive forms for *ich* (I), *er/sie/es* (he/she/it) and the same form for *wir* (we), *sie* (they) and *Sie* (polite 'you', both singular and plural).

In the <u>Present Tense</u> these endings are:

		e.g.:
ich	−*e*	*ich komme* (I come/am coming)
er/sie/es	−*t*	*er kommt* (he comes/is coming)
wir/sie/Sie	−*en*	*wir kommen* (we come/are coming)

Note, that there is only one form in German for he comes/is coming/does come: *er kommt.*

Since German nouns have a grammatical gender, i.e. they can be masculine or feminine as well as neuter, *er* and *sie* can also meant 'it'.

er kommt can mean a) **he** is coming
→ *Herr Müller kommt.*
(Mr Miller is coming.)

or   b) **it** is coming

→ *Der Bus kommt.*

(The bus is coming.)

sie kommt can mean a) **she** is coming

→ *Frau Müller kommt.*

(Mrs Miller is coming.)

or   b) **it** is coming

→ *Die Straßenbahn kommt.*

(The tram is coming.)

The main <u>*Past Tense*</u> form used in spoken German is formed with auxiliary verbs.

	II		END POSITION
Ich	*bin*	*mit dem Zug*	*gekommen.*
Er	*ist*	*mit dem Auto*	*gekommen.*
In Düsseldorf	*habe*	*ich Bier*	*getrunken.*
Er	*hat*	*Wein*	*getrunken.*

I came by train.
He came by car.

In Dusseldorf I drank beer.
He drank wine.

Translated literally the above sentences read:
I have/He has come/drunk....)

Note that in German you can say:

Seit 10 Jahren wohne ich in England.
For 10 years I live in England. → I *have been* living....

Instead of a <u>*Future Tense*</u> the Present Tense is often used:

Nächstes Jahr komme ich nach England.
Next year I come to England. → I *shall come....*

SOME FREQUENTLY USED VERBS

Forms of 'to be'

	Present	Past	
ich	*bin*	*war*	I am / was
er/sie/es	*ist*	*war*	he/she/it is/was
wir/sie/Sie	*sind*	*waren*	we/they/you are/were

e.g.: *Er ist heute in Berlin. Gestern war er in Frankfurt.*
He is in Berlin today. Yesterday he was in Frankfurt.

Forms of 'to have'

	Present	Past	
ich	*habe*	*hatte*	I have/had
er/sie/es	*hat*	*hatte*	He/she/it has/had
wir/sie/Sie	*haben*	*hatten*	we/they/you have/had

e.g.: *Jetzt habe ich Zeit. Heute morgen hatte ich keine Zeit.*
I have time now. This morning I did not have time.

Forms of 'to have to, must'

	Present	Past	
ich/er/sie/es	*muß*	*mußte*	I/he/she/it have/has to, had to
wir/sie/Sie	*müssen*	*mußten*	we/they/you have to, had to

e.g.: *Er muß nach Hamburg fahren.*
He has to/must go to Hamburg.

→ Word order: *fahren* is in the end position!

Note: *muß + nicht* does **not** mean 'must not', but 'does not have to' = 'need not'

Forms of 'to want/wish/intend to'

	Present	Past	
ich/er/sie/es	will	wollte	I/he/she/it want/s to, wanted to
wir/sie/Sie	wollen	wollten	we/they/you want to, wanted to

e.g.: *Sie will in Köln den Dom sehen.*
      She wants to see the cathedral in Cologne.

Forms of 'to be allowed to, to have permission'

	Present	Past	
ich/er/sie/es	darf	durfte	I/he/she/it am/is, was allowed to
wir/sie/Sie	dürfen	durften	we/they/you are, were allowed to

e.g.: *Darf ich hier rauchen?*
      May I / Am I allowed to smoke here?

Note: *darf + nicht* means 'must not'.

2

Pronunciation

Words never run into the next one

The following information on pronunciation is a rough guide only. To get the pronunciation of German words exactly right you need to listen to native speakers and to copy their way of speaking.

German words are pronounced exactly as they are spelt. Once you know the sound each letter or group of letters represent you can articulate each word clearly. In German endings are never slurred and words never run into the next one.

Note the following differences in pronunciation between English and German:

Consonants:

ch   After a, au, o, u it is pronounced like the 'ch' in the Scottish 'loch', in all other cases it corresponds to the 'H' in 'Hugh'.
       acht (eight)
       ich (I)

chs	When the 's' is part of the word itself (i.e. not simply linking two parts of a compound word) this is pronounced like an 'x' in English. *sechs* (six)
g	Is like the English hard 'g'. But after 'i' it is pronounced like 'H' in 'Hugh'. *gut* (good) *Pfennig* (penny)
j	Corresponds to the English 'y' *ja* (yes)
r	There is no exact equivalent in English. It very roughly corresponds to the 'r' in 'rice', but more trilled. *Reis* (reis)
sch	Corresponds to sh *Schiff* (ship)
sp,st	This is pronounced 'shp'/'sht' at the beginning of a word *Speisekarte* (menu) *Straße* (street)
th	Always pronounced as 't'. *Apotheke* (pharmacy)
v	Is pronounced like the English 'f'. *Vater* (father)
w	Is pronounced like the English 'v'. *Wahl* (vote)
z	Is pronounced like the English 'ts' as in 'tsar'. *Zug* (train)

Vowels can sound short or long:

a	As the 'a' in 'park' Short: *dann* (then) Long: *Tal* (valley)
e	As the 'e' in 'end'. Short: *Bett* (bed) Long: *wer* (who)

i	Is pronounced like 'ee'.
	Short: *Indien* (India)
	Long: *Chile* (Chile)
o	As the 'o' in 'hot'
	Short: *Post* (post)
	Long: *Pol* (pole)
u	As 'oo' in 'school'
	Short: *Universität* (university)
	Long: *Ufer* (river bank, shore)

Vowels with an *UMLAUT*:

ä	Is pronounced like 'ai' in 'air'.
	Short: *Äpfel* (apples)
	Long: *spät* (late)
ö	Is pronounced like the 'u' in 'fur'
	Short: *Köln* (Cologne)
	Long: *Börse* (wallet, purse, stock-exchange)
ü	There is no English equivalent. Pronounce it like 'ee' but with rounded lips.
	Short: *fünf* (five)
	Long: *für* (for)

Vowel Combinations:

au	Is pronounced like 'ow' in 'how'.
	Frau (woman, Mrs)
äu/eu	Is pronounced like 'oy' in 'boy'.
	Fräulein (Miss, waitress)
	Freude (joy)
ei	Is pronounced like 'i' in 'fine'.
	fein (fine)
ie	Is pronounced like 'e' in 'me'. Sometimes, however, i and e are pronounced as separate letters:
	die (the)
	Indien (India)

Arriving in Germany

Paßkontrolle

At the *Paßkontrolle* (passport control):
Ihren Paß, bitte! (Your passport, please.)

Occasionally you may be asked:
Wie lange bleiben Sie in Deutschland?
(How long will you be staying in Germany?)

einen Tag	(one day)
zwei/drei Tage	(two/three days)
eine Woche	(one week)
zwei/drei Wochen	(two/three weeks)
einen Monat	(one month)
zwei/drei Monate	(two/three months)

You may wish to add:
Ich bin geschäftlich hier (I am here on business.)
Ich bin hier auf Urlaub (I am here on holiday.)

A customs official may ask you:
Haben Sie etwas zu verzollen?
(Do you have something to declare?)

If you have nothing to declare reply: *Nein, [ich habe nichts zu verzollen.]*

Travelling by car, you may be asked for several documents:
Ihre Papiere, bitte! Paß (passport), *Führerschein* (driving licence), *grüne Versicherungskarte* (the green insurance card).

Arriving at an airport or station you may wish to take a *Taxi*. The driver will ask you:
Wohin bitte? (Where do you wish to go?)
Zum Hotel . . ., bitte! (To the . . . Hotel, please.)
Zum Stadtzentrum, bitte! (To the city centre, please.)
Zur . . . straße, bitte! (To . . . street/road, please.)
Nach . . ., bitte! (To [name of town/suburb etc], please.)
Was macht das, bitte? (How much is it, please?)

If you want to give a tip round up the amount to the nearest respectable full figure to allow for a tip of 5-10 per cent.

Say: *Das stimmt so!* (Literally: This is correct. Meaning of course the difference is for you.)

If you wish to hire a care look for the *Autoverleih* or *Mietwagen*.

Ich möchte |einen Wagen| mieten, bitte.
* |ein Auto |*
(I wish to hire a car.)

Car rental desks at airports are usually manned by English speakers and often the forms you have to fill in are both in German and English.

At the Hotel

Bavarian Inn Sign

If you have booked a room in advance:
Ich habe ein Zimmer reserviert. Mein Name ist...

(I have booked a room. My name is ...)

If you have not booked in advance:
Haben Sie Zimmer frei? (Do you have rooms free?)

The reply may be negative:
Nein, | *leider nicht.*
wir haben keine Zimmer frei.
wir sind voll ausgebucht.

If the answer is *Ja* (yes):

Ich möchte ein	*Einzelzimmer* *Doppelzimmer*	*mit*	*Bad.* *Dusche.* *Balkon.* *Telefon.* *Fernseher.*
I would like a	single room double room	with	bathroom. shower. balcony. telephone. television.

Was kostet ein . . . zimmer mit . . . ?
(How much is a . . . room with . . . ?)
Ist das inklusive Frühstück?
(Does this include breakfast?)
If you have asked for a double room:
Ist das pro Person oder pro Zimmer?
(Is this per room or per person?)

When you have made up your mind:
Ich nehme das Zimmer. (I'll take the room.)

You may be asked for how long you will want to stay:

Wir lange möchten Sie bleiben? or *Für wie lange?*

(*Für*)	*eine Nacht.*	(for one night)
	zwei Nächte	(two nights)
	eine Woche	(one week)
	zwei Wochen	(two weeks)

Bis Montag, Dienstag, Mittwoch, Donnerstag, Freitag, Samstag/Sonnabend, Sonntag.
(Until Monday, Tuesday, Wednesday, Thursday, Friday, Saturday, Sunday.)

Bis zum 14 April. (Until 14 April.)
→ REFERENCE SECTION

You are given the key: *(Hier ist) Ihr Schlüssel.*

The working day in Germany starts very early so you may wish to ask:

Wann gibt es Frühstück? (When is breakfast served?)
The reply may be:

Von 7 Uhr bis 9 Uhr. (From 7 until 9 o'clock.)
→ REFERENCE SECTION

The traditional breakfast in hotels consists of

Kaffee oder Tee	(coffee or tea)
ein weichgekochtes Ei	(a soft boiled egg)
Aufschnitt	(a selection of cold sliced meat/sausage)
Käse	(cheese)
Brot/Brötchen	(bread/bread rolls; usually several varieties)
Butter	(butter)
Marmelade	(jam. 'Marmalade' is called *Orangenmarmelade)*
Orangensaft	(orange juice)

In many hotels you help yourself from a buffet where cereals, yoghurts, fruit etc. are also available.

If you wish to make use of the services of the *Zimmerkellner* (Room service):

Bringen Sie mir bitte . . . auf Zimmer Nummer . . .
(Please bring . . . to room number . . .)

Finally, when you are leaving the hotel:

Meine Rechnung, bitte! (My bill, please.)

Meeting People

Greetings of the Day.

When meeting people it is the custom to shake hands. This applies not only to the very first meeting but to all subsequent ones. On leaving once again hands are shaken.

Being greeted with:

	Morgen!	in the morning
Guten	*Tag!*	at any time during the day
	Abend!	from early evening onwards

reply by repeating the greeting.

In Southeast Germany and Austria: *Grüb Gott!*
In Switzerland: *Grüezi!*

When leaving people say:
      Auf Wiedersehen! [Sometimes also: *Auf Wiederschauen!*] (Polite)
      Tschüs! (Informal)

INTRODUCING YOURSELF

Introduce yourself with

Mein Name ist	...[First	My name is ...
Ich heiße	name and	I am called ...
Ich bin	surname]	I am ...

If you are in Germany on business:
Ich bin von der Firma . . . in . . .
I am with/from [name of company] in . . .

If you have an appointment and you are reporting to reception:
Ich habe einen Termin mit Herrn/Frau . . . um . . . Uhr.
(I have an appointment with . . . at . . . o'clock.)
→ TIME: REFERENCE SECTION

When Germans introduce themselves they often simply say their surname, e.g.:

Guten Tag. Schneider.
The reply would be: . . . [Your surname] . . .
Guten Tag.
People sometimes say: *Freut mich!* or *Angenehm!* (Pleased to meet you!) when someone has introduced him/herself.

You may wish to say where you come from:

Ich komme aus	I come from
Großbritannien	Great Britain
England	England
Schottland	Scotland
den USA	the USA
Australien	Australia
Japan	Japan
Malaysia	Malaysia
Singapur	Singapore
Frankreich	France
Italien	Italy
Spanien	Spain

People might ask you some polite questions. There are polite standard replies which avoid you being questioned further:

Wie geht es Ihnen?   Reply: *(Sehr) gut, danke!*
How are you?   (Very) well, thank you!

Hatten Sie eine gute Reise? Ja, danke!
or *Wie war die Reise:*   *(Sehr) gut, danke!*
Did you have a good journey?   Yes, thank you.
or How was your journey?   Fine (Excellent),
                                          thank you.

Gefällt Ihnen | *Deutschland? Ja. (sehr) Es ist sehr*
                  Österreich   schön/
                  die Schweiz?   interessant
                  Berlin?
                  Hamburg?

Do you like Germany/Austria/   Yes, (very much). It is
   Switzerland etc?   very nice/interesting.

INTRODUCING OTHERS

Das ist | *(mein Kollege)* | *Herr . . .[Surname]*
           | *(meine Kollegin)* | *Frau. . .*
           | | *Herr/Frau D[okto]r. . .*
This is | (my colleague) | Mr. . .
           | | Mrs/Miss/Ms. . .
           | | Dr. . .

Giving Information/ Talking about Yourself

Family photo

On forms you may have to fill in:

Nachname/Familienname	Surname
Vorname(n)	First name(s)
Adresse: Wohnort	town/city/village
Straße	street
Hausnummer	house number
Telefonnummer	telephone number
Geburtsdatum	date of birth
Geburtsort	place of birth
Staatsangehörigkeit	nationality
Beruf	occupation

G ermans tend to keep their private life and business apart. However, when meeting socially you may wish to talk about your family and your private interests. If you are showing photographs of your family:

Das ist meine	*Frau.*	This is my	wife.
	Tochter.		daughter.
	Mutter.		mother.
	Schwester.		sister.
mein	*Mann.*		husband.
	Sohn.		son.
	Vater.		father.
	Bruder.		brother.

Das sind meine	*Töchter.*	These are my	daughters.
	Söhne.		sons.
	Kinder.		children.
	Brüder.		brothers.
	Schwestern.		sisters.

Er / Sie ist . . . [Jahre alt]. He/She is . . . [years old]
→ NUMBERS: REFERENCE SECTION

T alking about your hobbies:

Ich spiele (gern)	*Tennis*	I [like to] play	tennis.
	Golf		golf.
	Kricket.		cricket.
	Fußball.		football.
	Klavier.		piano.

Ich laufe (gern) Ski. I do (like) skiing.

Ich	*schwimme*	*gern.*	I like	swimming.
	wandere			walking.

Ich arbeite gern im Garten. I like gardening.

On the Telephone

Ich rufe später an.

When looking up a number in a German telephone directory note that since German is an inflected language entries appear in an order different to an English one. For example *Deutsche Lufthansa* is listed before *Deutscher Hof*.

When answering the phone either give your name or telephone number, or room number, if you are staying in a hotel.

→ NUMBERS: REFERENCE SECTION

If the caller asks to speak to you:

Am Apparat. (Speaking.)

Asking to be put through to

an extension: | *Apparat . . ., bitte!* (Ext . . ., please.)
a person: | *Herr/Frau . . ., bitte!*

or more formally:

Ich möchte Herrn/Frau . . . sprechen, bitte!
(I would like to speak to . . ., please!)

You may be told that the line is engaged: *Der Apparat ist besetzt.*

If the person you wish to talk to is not available you may be told:

...ist | *nicht im Haus.* (. . . is not in the building.)
| *in einer Besprechung.* (. . . is in a meeting.)
| *auf Urlaub.* (. . . is on holiday.)

You may be asked if you would like to leave a message:

Kann ich etwas ausrichten?

You may prefer to ring back later. Say:

Ich rufe später an. Wann ist Herr/Frau . . . im Hause?
(I'll call back later. When will Mr/Mrs/Miss/Ms . . . be in?)
→ TIME: REFERENCE SECTION

If you wish to make an appointment:

Ich möchte einen Termin mit Herrn/Frau . . .
(I would like to make an appointment with . . .)
→ DAYS OF THE WEEK, DATES etc:
REFERENCE SECTION

You may be asked to spell your name:

Wie buchstabiert man ihren Namen, bitte?
(How is your name spelt?)
→ SPELLING: REFERENCE SECTION

On the phone a special version of 'Goodbye' is used:
Auf Wiederhören!
(Literally: Until we hear each other again.)
Reply by repeating it.

In the Restaurant

Prost! / Zum Wohl!

Inviting somebody for a meal/drinks:

Darf ich Sie zum	*Mittagessen*	*einladen?*
	Abendessen	
	zu einem Drink	
May I invite you for	lunch?	
	dinner?	
	drinks?	

The reply might be:
Ja, gern. Das wäre sehr nett!
Thank you. It is very kind of you.

However, the person may be busy: *Nein, danke. Ich habe leider keine Zeit.*

If you are in Germany on business, endeavouring to sell a product or an idea, you will be expected to do the entertaining. This means not only picking up the bill, but also making the arrangements, i.e. booking a table etc.

You may first have to find out where there is a good restaurant.

Können Sie ein gutes | *Restaurant* | *empfehlen?*
| *Lokal* |
(Can you recommend a good restaurant?)

S ince Germany is a multicultural society as far as eating and drinking is concerned, you may be asked what kind of food you like:

Was essen Sie denn gern?
Ich esse gern | *chinesisch.*   (Chinese)
| *französisch.*   (French)
| *italienisch.*   (Italian)
| *griechisch.*   (Greek)
| *deutsch.*   (German)

You may need to reserve a table:

Ich möchte einen Tisch reservieren für
    eine Person | *um . . . Uhr.*
    zwei Personen |
    vier Personen |
(I would like to book a table for one/two/four, at . . . o'clock.)   → TIME: REFERENCE SECTION

When you arrive at the restaurant:

Ich habe einen Tisch reserviert. Mein Name ist . . .
(I have booked a table. My name is . . .)

If you have not booked in advance:

Haben Sie einen Tisch für . . . Personen?
(Have you got a table for . . .?)

If you have to find a table yourself and it seems that you have to share a table:

Entschuldigung, ist hier noch frei?
(Excuse me, is this seat/are these seats free?)

Calling for the waiter/waitress: *Herr Ober/ Fräulein, bitte!*
Asking for the menu/wine list: *Die Speisekarte/ Weinkarte, bitte!*

Words you might find on the menu:

Vorspeisen	hors d'oeuvre, starter
Hauptgerichte	main dishes
Nachspeisen	desserts
Suppen	soups
Fleischgerichte:	meat dishes:
Schwein....	pork
Rind....	beef
Kalb....	veal
Reh....	venison
Hähnchen....	chicken
Geflügel....	poultry
Schnitzel....	a kind of cutlet without bones
Fischgerichte: Forelle	fish dishes: trout
Eierspeisen: Spiegeleier	egg dishes: fried egg
Rühreier	scrambled egg
Omelett	omelette
(gemischte) Salate	(mixed) salad
Kartoffeln: Pommes Frites	potatoes: chips
Röstkartoffeln	sauté potatoes
Salzkartoffeln	boiled potatoes
Kroketten	croquettes
Reis	rice
Teigwaren oder Nudeln	pasta
Spaghetti	spaghetti
Spätzle	South German pasta speciality
Gemüse: Bohnen	vegetables: beans
Erbsen	peas
Karotten	carrots
Pilze:	
Champignons	mushrooms
Tomaten	tomatoes
Käse	cheese
Eis	ice cream
Obstsalat	fruit salad

Bedienung und Mehrwertsteuer inbegriffen/inklusive.	Service and VAT included

Getränke:

Tasse	*Kaffee*	cup of | coffee or tea
Kännchen	*oder Tee*	pot
Mineralwasser		mineral water
Apfelsaft		apple juice
Bier: Pils		beer: 2 kinds of German
Export		lager
Wein: Rotwein		wine: red wine
Weißwein		white wine
Sekt		champagne
Weinbrand		brandy
Whisky		whisky

W hen you are ready to order tell the waiter:
Ich möchte jetzt bestellen, bitte.

Ich möchte bitte....   I would like....
or if you are ordering the same dish for several people:

Zweimal....	....twice
Dreimal....	....three times
Viermal....	....four times

The waiter/waitress may ask you whether you want a particular dish <u>with</u> or <u>without</u> additional items:

Möchten Sie Eis <u>mit</u> oder <u>ohne</u> Sahne?

Before ordering wine you may wish to ask whether it is a dry or sweet wine:

Ist dieser Wein trocken oder süß?

eine Flasche Wein	a bottle of wine
ein Glas Bier	a glass of beer

B efore starting to drink Germans raise their glasses and say:

Zum Wohl!   Cheers!
or *Prost!*

Before starting to eat Germans say: *Guten Appetit!*
The reply to this is: *Danke, gleichfalls!*

After you have finished your meal the waiter/waitress usually asks if you have enjoyed your meal:

Hat es geschmeckt?

If you have enjoyed it the reply is simply:

Ja danke.

Asking for the bill: *Die Rechnung, bitte!*

The waiter/waitress may ask: *Zusammen oder getrennt?* (Together or separate?)

If you want to give a tip simply round up the amount to the nearest respectable figure allowing for a tip of around 5-10% and when handing over the money say:

Das stimmt so! (This is for you.)

9

Getting About

USING PUBLIC TRANSPORT

In order to find your way around you may want to buy a streetplan or map:

Ich möchte | einen Stadtplan | von . . .,
 | eine Landkarte | bitte.
 | eine Straßenkarte |

(I would like [to buy] a streetplan/map/road map of . . . please.)

Germany has an extensive public transport network. As well as trains *[Züge]* and buses *[Busse]* many cities also have trams *[Straßenbahnen]*, and/or underground trains *[U-Bahnen]* and/or high-speed city railways *[Schnellbahnen]*.

(City) sightseeing tours are called *(Stadt)-rundfahrt* and the local tourist information office *[Verkehrsamt/Verkehrsverein/Touristen Information]* will have details.

If you prefer to explore the city by taxi look out for a *Taxistand* (taxi rank).

Tickets *[Fahrkarten]* for the Federal Railways can be bought in travel agents *[Reisebüro]* as well as, of course, the (main)station *[(Haupt)bahnhof]*.

Tickets for trips on local public transport usually have to be bought before getting on. You can buy them from ticket machines *[Fahrkartenautomat]*, special ticket kiosks and sometimes from newsagents with special licences to sell tickets.

As you board the bus, tram, etc. you need to cancel your ticket in an *Entwerter* (a ticket cancelling machine). You may prefer to buy a *Sammelfahrschein* (a ticket allowing you to make several trips). Tickets which allow you to travel during a specified time *[Zeitkarte]* are also available in many cities.

Buying tickets at a counter:

Einmal	..[DESTINATION]..	*einfach*	, bitte.
Zweimal		*hin und*	
		zurück	

(One ticket to . . . single, please.
Two tickets to . . . return.)

If you want to reserve a seat on a train: *Ich möchte einen Platz reservieren*. You may be asked: *Wann fahren Sie?* (When are you travelling?) *Am* ..[date].. *um* . . . [time].

→ DATES/TIME etc: REFERENCE SECTION and whether you prefer a smoking or non-smoking seat:

Raucher oder Nichtraucher and if you would like a window seat: *ein Fensterplatz*.

You may need to ask someone where a particular train/tram/boat is going to:

Wohin fährt	*dieser Zug?*
	diese Straßenbahn?
	dieses Schiff?

Or if it is going to the place you wish to go:
Fährt dieser Zug nach . . .?
(Is this train going to . . .?)

You may need to ask about departure times and place of departure:

Wann fährt	*der nächste Bus*	*nach. . .?*
	die nächste	
	Straßenbahn	
	das nächste Schiff	

(When does the next bus/tram/boat leave for . . . ?)
→ TIME: REFERENCE SECTION

Wo fährt der Bus nach . . . ab?
(From where does the bus to . . . depart?)

You may have to ask whether you have to change trains/buses etc:

Muß ich umsteigen?

If you prefer to buy a time-table: *Einen Fahrplan, bitte!*

ASKING WHERE SOMETHING IS SITUATED

Entschuldigung!   Excuse me!

Wo	*ist*	*Gleis . . .*	*, bitte?*
		die Straßenbahnhaltestelle	
		der Bahnhof	
		der Wartesaal	
		der Informationsschalter	
		die Gepäckaufbewahrung	
	sind	*die Toiletten*	

Where	is	platform . . .	please?
		the tram stop	
		the station	
		the waiting room	
		the information desk	
		the left luggage office	
	are	the toilets	

Listen for these key words:

rechts	on the right	*neben*	next to / beside
links	on the left	*gegenüber*	opposite
geradeaus	straight on	*vor*	in front of / before
oben	above / up	*hinter*	behind
unten	below / down	*zwischen*	between
in der Mitte	in the centre		

im	*ersten / zweiten / dritten Stock*
	Erdgeschoß
	Untergeschoß
on the	first / second / third floor
	ground floor
in the	basement

ASKING THE WAY

Wie komme ich (von hier)	How do I get (from here)
zum Bahnhof?	to the station?
zur Kathedrale?	to the cathedral?
zum Rathaus?	to the town/city hall?
zur . . . straße	to the . . . street?
zum . . . Platz?	to the . . . square?
nach . . .?	to . . . [place name]?

Listen out for these key words and phrases:

Gehen	*Sie bis zur/zum*	*Eck.*
Fahren		*Kreuzung.*
		Ampel.
		Brücke.
		Treppe.
		Fußgängerzone.

		Kirche.
		Parkplatz.
		Hauptstraße.
	ersten	*Seitenstraße.*
		Querstraße.

Walk	until you come to the	corner.
Drive	as far as the	crossroads.
		traffic lights.
		bridge.
		stairs/steps.
		pedestrian precinct.
		church.
		car park.
		main street.
		first side street.
		first road at right angles to the one you are on.

| *Biegen Sie* | *links* *rechts* | *ab.* | Turn | left right. |

| *den Berg* | *hinauf* *hinunter.* | up down | the hill |

| *über die Brücke* | across the bridge |

| *die Straße entlang* | follow the road |

Y ou may want to know how far it is:

Wie weit ist das	*zu Fuß?*
	mit dem Auto/Bus?
How far is it	on foot?
	by car/bus?

Nicht sehr weit.	Not very far.
Etwa zehn Minuten.	About ten minutes.
Das ist ganz in der Nähe.	It is quite close.

TRAVELLING BY CAR

A t the petrol station *[die Tankstelle]* if it is not one of the self-service ones:

Volltanken, bitte.	Fill her up, please.
Zwanzig Liter, bitte.	Twenty litres, please.
Super	Four star petrol.
Bleifrei	Lead free petrol.

Some jobs you may wish the petrol station attendant to see to:

Kontrollieren Sie bitte	*den Ölstand.*
	den Reifendruck.
Please check	the oil.
	the tyre pressure.

Füllen Sie bitte das Wasser nach.
Please top up the water.

You may want to have your car washed:

Wo ist die (Auto)waschanlage?
Where is the car wash?

The petrol station attendant may wish you a safe journey: *Gute Fahrt!*

You may need to take the car for repairs to a garage *[eine (Reparatur)werkstatt]*. The word *Garage* is only used for the place you leave the car at night.

10

Shopping

Note that Eurocheques *[Euroschecks]* are widely accepted but that not all shops accept credit cards. If they do, a sign displaying the logo of the card can be seen at the entrance to the shop.

FOOD SHOPPING

In the *Supermarkt* you will, of course find all basic food items. If you cannot see what you want to buy ask:

Haben Sie . . .? Do you have . . .?

You may prefer to go to specialist food shops:

die Bäckerei	baker
die Metzgerei / Fleischerei	butcher
das Obst- und Gemüsegeschäft	greengrocer

In Germany weight is measured in grammes *[Gramm]* and kilogrammes *[Kilo(gramm)]*.

→ WEIGHTS: REFERENCE SECTION

For example:

Einhundert Gramm Schinken, bitte	100 g of ham please
Ein halbes Kilo Bananen, bitte.	½ kg bananas please.

Asking for the price: *Was kostet das?*

→ NUMBERS: REFERENCE SECTION

When asking for a specific item, say:

Ich möchte . . .   I would like . . .

If you do not like what you are being shown:
Nein, danke!   Thank you, no.

If it is too expensive, say:
Das ist zu teuer!

SOME ITEMS YOU MAY WISH TO BUY

At the Newsagent:
Ich möchte:

eine	*englische* *amerikanische*	*Zeitung*
an	English American	newspaper

einen Kugelschreiber (or short): *Kuli*	a ballpoint pen
einen Bleistift	a pencil
ein (Taschen)buch	(paperback) book
Ansichtskarten	picture postcards
Schreibpapier	note/letter paper
Papiertaschentücher	paper handkerchieves tissues
Zigaretten	cigarettes
Streichhölzer	matches
Kaugummi	chewing gum
Pfefferminz(bonbons)	peppermints (sweets)

At the Chemist:

eine Seife	a bar of soap
Zahnpasta	toothpaste
eine Zahnbürste	a tooth brush
Shampoo	shampoo
ein Duschgel	shower gel
ein Deodorant	a deodorant
eine Rasiercreme	shaving cream
ein Rasierwasser	aftershave
Kondome	condoms
Damenbinden	sanitary towels
Tampons	tampons
Parfüm	perfume
eine Packung	a packet of sticking-
Heftpflaster	plaster
eine Sonnenbrille	sunglasses
einen Schirm	an umbrella

CLOTHES, SHOES ETC

Some words and phrases you may need:

das	*Damen*	*geschäft*
die	*Herren*	*abteilung*
	Kinder	
	Schuh	

Shop selling clothes for ladies.

Department selling	clothes for	gentlemen.
		children
	shoes.	

Plural:

der Mantel	*die Mäntel*	coat/s
das Kleid	*die Kleider*	dress/es
der Pullover	*die Pullover*	pullover/s
die Hose	*die Hosen*	trousers
die Bluse	*die Blusen*	blouse/s
das Hemd	*die Hemden*	shirt/s
die Unterwäsche	—	underwear

If you want an item in a different size or colour:

Haben sie das größer?
                kleiner?
                in rot/gelb/schwarz/weiß/grün/
                blau/braun?

Do you have this in a larger size, smaller size, in red/yellow/
black/white/green/blue/brown?

Enquiring about the material:

Ist das aus Wolle/Baumwolle/Seide/Leder?
Is this made of wool/cotton/silk/leather?

11

At the Bank / Post Office

The following coins and banknotes are in circulation:

Münzen (coins):

    1 / 2 / 5 / 10 / 50 *Pfennig*

    1 / 2 / 5 *DM* (Deutsch Mark)

Scheine (notes):

    5 / 10 / 20 / 50 / 100 / 200 / 500 / 1000 *DM*

100 *Pfennig* = 1 *DM*

If you wish to cash traveller's cheques:

Ich möchte Reiseschecks einlösen, bitte.
I want to cash traveller's cheques, please.

If you want to change cash:

Ich möchte Geld wechseln, bitte.

You may be asked to sign your name:

Unterschreiben Sie hier, bitte.

Buying stamps:

..[NUMBER].. *Briefmarken für* ..[COUNTRY]..,
bitte.
. . . stamps for . . ., please.

If you want more colourful special stamps:

Sondermarken, bitte!

If your letter needs to be weighed:

Ich möchte diesen Brief nach . . . schicken.
I want to send this letter to . . .

If you need to send a telegram:

Ich möchte ein Telegramm schicken.

Post your letter where you see the sign
Briefeinwurf. Mailboxes are painted yellow.

Going to the Theatre / Cinema / Concert

The Golden Bear award
Berlin Film Festival

Was wird im	*Kino*	*gezeigt?*
	Theater	*gespielt?*
	Konzertsaal	
What is on at the	cinema?	
	theatre?	
	concert hall?	

You can buy tickets *[Karten]* at the advance booking office *[Im Vorverkauf]* or at the door/box office *[An der Abendkasse]*.

. . . Karten für ..[title of play/film etc].
. . . tickets for . . .

You will be asked:

Wo möchten Sie sitzen? Where would you like to sit?

Im	*Parkett*		stalls
	ersten	*Rang*	dress circle
	zweiten		upper circle
	dritten		gallery

Reihe . . .	row . . .
Mitte	centre
Seite	side

When Things Go Wrong

AT THE CHEMIST

In Germany there are *Apotheken* which sell medicines only and *Drogerien* which sell a wide range of goods: cosmetics, films etc.

Ich möchte etwas gegen I would like something for

Kopfschmerzen	headaches
Halsschmerzen	sore throat
Magenschmerzen	stomach ache
Durchfall	diarrhoea
Verstopfung	constipation
Hühneraugen	corns

AT THE DOCTOR / DENTIST

A *Praktischer Arzt* (male doctor) / *Ärztin* (female doctor) deals with all illnesses. You can also go directly to a specialist. For example:

ein Augenarzt	eye specialist
ein Hals-, Nasen- und Ohrenarzt	ear, nose and throat specialist

ein Arzt für innere   specialist for internal
  Krankheiten   illnesses

On the sign outside the doctor's surgery:

Sprechstunden (consulting hours)
täglich von . . . (daily from . . .)
   → DAYS OF WEEK/TIME: REFERENCE SECTION

You may have to make an appointment:

Ich möchte einen Termin, bitte.
I would like an appointment, please.

The doctor may ask you:
Was fehlt Ihnen? OR Wo tut es weh?
What is the matter/what is wrong? OR Where does it hurt?

Pointing to the place where it hurts:
Hier tut es weh!

The doctor may ask you since when you have
had this complaint: *Seit wann?*

S/he may refer you to the hospital *[das
Krankenhaus]* for X-rays *[zum Röntgen]*.

The dentist is called *Zahnarzt*, toothache is
Zahnschmerzen.

AT THE POLICE STATION

You may have to report to the police *[die
Polizei]* that something has been damaged
or stolen:

Jemand hat	
meinen Photoapparat	*gestohlen.*
meine Uhr	
mein Auto	*beschädigt.*
Somebody has	
stolen	my camera.
	my watch.
damaged	my car.

You may wish to ask for assistance:

Ich möchte	*einen Rechtsanwalt*
	mit dem Konsulat telefonieren.
I would like	a solicitor
	to call the consulate.

14

Summary of Basic Words and Phrases

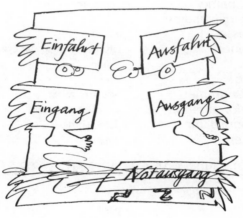

Ins and outs

SIGNS TO RECOGNISE

Ausgang	exit [on foot]
Ausfahrt	exit [for vehicles]
Notausgang	emergency exit
Eingang	entrance [on foot]
Einfahrt	entrance [for vehicles]

kein and **nicht** signal **NO**

Kein *Eingang*,	
Kein *Zugang*	= NO entry
Nicht*raucher*	= NON-smoker

Verboten	Prohibited
Umleitung	Diversion
Polizei	Police
Zoll	Customs

Toiletten / WC	toilets
Damen / Herren or *D / H*	Ladies / Gentlemen
Besetzt	engaged
Frei	free

WORDS ON FORMS

Vorname	first name
Nachname/ Familienname	surname
Adresse	address
Wohnort	city/town/village where you live
Straße	street
Hausnummer	house number
Telefonnummer	telephone number
Geburtsdatum	date of birth
Datum	date

ESSENTIAL WORDS AND PHRASES TO LEARN

Ja	yes
Nein	no
Bitte (Bitte schön)	please

Make sure you use this word. Without it most requests and questions sound too abrupt.

This word is also used for 'Don't mention it./It's a pleasure' (and by shop assistants with the meaning 'Can I help you?')

Danke (or *Danke sehr / Danke schön / Vielen Dank)*	Thank you
Guten Morgen	Good morning
Guten Tag	Greeting which can be used throughout the day
Guten Abend	Good evening
Gute Nacht	Good night
Auf Wiedersehen	Good bye
Entschuldigung / Verzeihung	I am sorry. Excuse me.

Wie bitte?	I beg your pardon?
Sprechen Sie Englisch?	Do you speak English?
Ich verstehe (das) nicht.	I don't understand.
Was heißt das auf Englisch?	What does this mean in English?

When asking for things or for something to be done you only need to learn one phrase:

Ich möchte . . .

e.g.

Ich möchte	*ein Einzelzimmer mit Bad.*
	Herrn/Frau . . . sprechen.
	einen Termin
	Reiseschecks einlösen.
I would like	a single room with bath.
	to speak to Mr/Mrs/Miss . . .
	an appointment.
	to cash traveller's cheques.

Mein Name ist . . .	My name is . . .
Ich habe einen Termin mit....	I have an appointment with....

Asking questions:

Was kostet das . . .?	How much is . . .?
Wo ist . . .?	Where is . . .?
Wohin fährt diese/r/s . . .?	Where is this . . . going to?
Wann . . .?	When . . .?
Haben Sie . . .?	Do you have . . .?
Ist hier noch frei?	Is this seat/table still unoccupied?
Einmal . . . einfach, bitte.	One single ticket to . . ., please.
hin und zurück	return

In the Taxi:

Zum Hotel . . ., bitte.	To the hotel . . ., please.
Nach . . ., bitte	To . . . [name of town/ suburb] . . ., please.
Die Rechnung, bitte!	The bill, please.

mit / ohne	with / without
e.g. *Kaffee mit Milch und Zucker*	coffee with milk and sugar
Guten Appetit!	This is said before starting a meal.
Prost! OR Zum Wohl!	Cheers!

WORDS AND PHRASES YOU MAY HEAR

Bitte nehmen Sie Platz!	Please take a seat.
Viel Spaß / Viel Vergnügen!	Have fun! Enjoy yourself!
Gute Reise! / Gute Fahrt!	Bon voyage!
Guten Aufenthalt!	Have a nice stay!
Alles Gute!	All the best!
Frohe Weihnachten! / Frohe Ostern!	Happy Christmas/ Easter!

15

Reference Section

Radish seller

NUMBERS

0	*null*		
1	*eins*	11	*elf*
2	*zwei*	12	*zwölf*
3	*drei*	13	*dreizehn*
4	*vier*	14	*vierzehn*
5	*fünf*	15	*fünfzehn*
6	*sechs*	16	*sechzehn*
7	*sieben*	17	*siebzehn*
8	*acht*	18	*achtzehn*
9	*neun*	19	*neunzehn*
10	*zehn*	20	*zwanzig*
21	*einundzwanzig*	80	*achtzig*
29	*neunundzwanzig*	90	*neunzig*
30	*dreißig*	100	*(ein)hundert*
40	*vierzig*	200	*zweihundert*
50	*fünfzig*	900	*neunhundert*
60	*sechzig*	1,000	*(ein)tausend*
70	*siebzig*		

1,456 *eintausend-vierhundert-sechs-und-fünfzig*

1st =	1.	*der/die/das erst...*
2nd =	2.	*zweit...*
3rd =	3.	*dritt...*
4th =	4.	*viert...*
19th =	19.	*neunzehnt...*
20th =	20.	*zwanzigst...*

½ *(ein)halb, die Hälfte*
¼ *ein Viertel*

Note in German a comma is used instead of a decimal point: 2,5

20,45 DM *zwanzig Mark fünfundvierzig (Pfennig)*
 0,30 DM *dreißig Pfennig*

WEIGHTS AND MEASURES

1000 g *(Gramm)* = 1 kg *(Kilogramm)*
100 cm *(Zentimeter)* = 1 m *(Meter)*
1000 cm^3 *(Kubikzentimeter)* = 1 l *(Liter)*

DAYS OF THE WEEK

Montag	Monday
Dienstag	Tuesday
Mittwoch	Wednesday
Donnerstag	Thursday
Freitag	Friday
Samstag/Sonnabend	Saturday
Sonntag	Sunday

MONTHS OF THE YEAR

Januar, Februar, März, April, Mai, Juni, Juli, August, September, Oktober, November, Dezember

DATES

e.g.: on 3 April 1992
am dritten April
  neunzehnhundertzweiundneunzig

THE TIME

The 24 hour clock is used for all official announcements:

8.30 am = *acht Uhr dreißig*
8.30 pm = *zwanzig Uhr dreißig*

There is, however, a German equivalent to half past/quarter to/past etc. With these forms the 12 hour clock only is used:

8.30 pm = *halb neun (Uhr)*, i.e.: half <u>to</u> the
            next full hour!
  NOTE THE DIFFERENCE TO THE ENGLISH FORM!

8.45 pm = *viertel **vor** neun (Uhr)*
            quarter <u>to</u> nine
            OR:
            fünfzehn Minuten vor neun (Uhr)
            fifteen minutes to nine
9.15 pm = *viertel **nach** neun (Uhr)*
            quarter <u>past</u> nine
            OR:
            fünfzehn Minuten nach neun (Uhr)
            fifteen minutes past nine

To clarify the time of day:

8.30 am = *halb neun (Uhr) **morgens*** [half past
            eight in the morning]
3.30 pm = *halb vier (Uhr) **nachmittags*** [half
            past three in the afternoon]
8.30 pm = *halb neun (Uhr) **abends*** [half past
            eight in the evening]

Wann ist der Informationsschalter geöffnet?
When is the information desk open?
Von *acht Uhr morgens* **bis** *sechs Uhr abends.*
From 8am **until** 6pm.

SPELLING

When asked to spell a word

Wie | *buchstabiert* | *man das?*   How is it | spelt | ?
    | *schreibt* | | written |
Buchstabieren Sie das bitte!   Please spell it.

Germans may use the
TELEPHONE ALPHABET

A	*wie* (as in)	*Anton*
Ä		*Ärger*
B		*Berta*
C		*Cäsar*
D		*Dora*
E		*Emil*
F		*Friedrich*
G		*Gustav*
H		*Heinrich*
I		*Ida*
J		*Julius*
K		*Kaufmann*
L		*Ludwig*
M		*Martha*
N		*Nordpol*
O		*Otto*
O		*Okonom*
P		*Paula*
Q		*Quelle*
R		*Richard*
S		*Samuel*
T		*Theodor*
U		*Ulrich*
U		*Ubermut*
V		*Viktor*
W		*Wilhelm*
X		*Xanthippe*
Y		*Ypsilon*
Z		*Zacharias*

For example someone might say:
Mein Name ist Meyer. Meyer mit E(MIL) / YPSILON.
My name is Meyer. Meyer spelt with ey.

Ich bin heute in Viersen. Viersen: VIKTOR IDA EMIL RICHARD SAMUEL EMIL NORDPOL.
I am in Viersen today. Viersen is spelt: VIERSEN

VOCAB /MEMO

VOCAB /MEMO